This 1988 edition published in the U.S.A. by Grosset & Dunlap,
a member of The Putnam Publishing Group, New York.
All rights reserved. Printed in Hong Kong.
Library of Congress Catalog Card Number: 87-81716
ISBN 0-448-19221-7
B C D E F G H I J
Rev. ed. of: OWL's Question & answer book #1 and
OWL's Question & answer book #2.
Includes index.

OWL Books are published in Canada by Greey de Pencier
Books, Toronto. OWL is a trademark of The Young
Naturalist Foundation. No part of this book may be
reproduced or copied in any form without written permission
from the publisher. © 1987 Greey de Pencier Books.

Edited by Katherine Farris
Art direction by Nick Milton

THE KIDS'
Question & Answer
BOOK

From the editors of OWL Magazine

GROSSET & DUNLAP · NEW YORK
A member of The Putnam Publishing Group

What was the smallest dinosaur?

The smallest dinosaur, Compsognathus, was no bigger than a chicken. The Compsognathus appeared about the same time as the first birds, more than 200 million years ago, and scientists think it might even have looked a bit like a wingless, featherless bird. It had a thin, bird-shaped body and walked on chickenlike hind feet. Although the Compsognathus was tiny compared to most of its relatives, sharp, flesh-ripping teeth and three-clawed front "arms" made it a dangerous predator of many smaller creatures.

How do we know what dinosaurs looked like?

Paleontologists, just like detectives, have pieced together dinosaurs' bones and have studied skin impressions in rocks. Many museums have special exhibits featuring dinosaurs, but scientists have recently discovered that some dinosaur bones have been put together incorrectly. Watch for changes in exhibits.

What dinosaur was the largest?

Diplodocus was the longest, about the length of two modern buses. But it wasn't as heavy as Brachiosaurus, which was shorter and about as high as a bus on end. Brachiosaurus was the "heavy," weighing about the same as nine full-grown elephants.

Were dinosaurs brightly colored?

The color of an animal fades very quickly after it dies, so it is impossible to tell from the remains that have been found buried in rocks what colors dinosaurs were.

How did dinosaurs have babies?

Because of the egg shells scientists have found, it is believed that dinosaurs laid eggs in shallow holes in the warm sand, then covered them and left them to hatch. Baby dinosaurs crawled out, just as young turtles and crocodiles do today.

How did dinosaurs die?

Something happened 65 million years ago that destroyed three-quarters of all life on earth – including dinosaurs. Was it a sudden catastrophe, or was it a long, slow process? Whatever it was, only plants, mouselike animals, birds and insects survived.

This riddle has long fascinated scientists. Perhaps sun flares or an exploding star bathed the earth in deadly radiation. Or maybe there was massive volcanic activity that produced so much dust that sunlight was blocked off. Or maybe the earth passed through a dust cloud, causing world temperatures to drop, or perhaps several events combined to bring about the mass extinction.

Most scientists now believe that most of the world's plants and animals died out slowly as a result of a gradual change in climate. They say that if part of each year started to get very cold, only those creatures able to adapt – for example, warm-blooded animals with fur or feathers for insulation – could have survived. Dinosaurs had neither fur nor feathers, so gradually they perished.

8

Did dinosaurs make noises?

No one really knows if dinosaurs made noises, but it is thought that the hollow crests on the heads of a family of dinosaurs called hadrosaurs contained an air passage from nose to throat where loud sounds were made. But these air passages could also have been used to improve the dinosaurs' sense of smell.

Did cavemen kill and eat dinosaurs?

Cavemen did not have anything to do with dinosaurs because the last one disappeared 60 million years before the first human appeared on earth. Dinosaurs, some of which were the largest animals ever to exist on earth, lived during what is called the Mesozoic era, which lasted from about 225 to 65 million years ago.

Did dragons ever really exist?

The dragons in our storybooks exist only in the minds of people, but they've been lurking there for thousands of years. Some of the oldest tales about dragons are the wildest. For example, would you believe that dragons were fond of cooling themselves on hot days by drinking chilled elephants' blood?

Where did people get all their odd ideas about dragons? No one knows, but whoever first saw a giant lizard leap out of underbrush on the South Pacific island of Komodo must have thought he had seen a storybook dragon in the flesh.

Komodo dragons, which weigh more than a full refrigerator and are

almost twice as long, lumber around on legs as thick as tree trunks and feed on wild pigs, deer and water buffalo. And like their distant snake

relatives, they sometimes swallow prey whole. Komodo dragons have been seen gulping down a pig, then walking off with their bellies dragging on the ground!

Is it true that crocodiles cry?

When somebody says a person is shedding crocodile tears, he or she means that person is pretending to be sad. This expression began because some people once believed that

crocodiles cried to make their victims come closer to see what was the matter. It is now known that crocodiles do cry, but for physical, rather than emotional reasons. Their kidneys are unable to get

rid of all the salt that crocodiles take in, so glands in their head extract the salt and pass it out as tears.

Penguins and other seabirds that eat salty food and drink mostly

salt water also must rid their bodies of salt, so they too have salt glands above their eyes. Their tears dribble down their bills and away.

How can alligators keep their eyes open underwater?

An alligator is very cleverly built for lying around in the water, which it likes to do. Its eyes and nostrils are on the top of its head so that it can breathe and also look around. When an alligator dives, it battens down its hatches like a submarine. Two flaps of muscle in each nostril clamp shut so the water doesn't flood its nose. Other muscle flaps close off an alligator's ears like internal earmuffs. Then it puts on its "goggles," a special transparent third eyelid that is only used underwater. No water can get through, and the eyelid is clear enough for the alligator to see where it's going.

How do you tell the difference between an alligator and a crocodile?

Fortunately you don't have to go too near to tell the difference. The alligator is the one with the broad head and rounded snout, while the crocodile is slimmer and has a long, narrow head and pointed snout. Also, crocodiles tend to be somewhat lighter in color.

If you are up close, there is another way to tell the difference. When its mouth is closed, none of an alligator's teeth stick out. But when a crocodile's mouth is closed, its long fourth side tooth on the lower jaw can be seen pointing up.

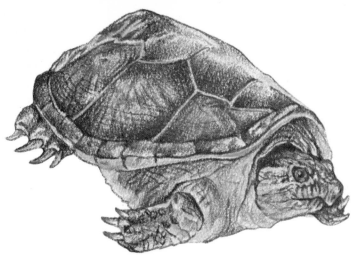

What do turtles eat?

A turtle eats whatever's in front of its beak. Some eat fish and water animals; others eat insects, worms and bits of dead animals; and some eat both plant and animal food. There are even some vegetarian turtles.

Some turtles start out life eating meat, which helps them to grow faster. In old age, however, the same turtle may be quite content to munch only on plants.

Turtles' eating habits are unusual in another way: with the exception of land turtles and snapping turtles, most will only swallow underwater.

What's the difference between frogs and toads?

The most obvious difference between these two amphibians is their skin. A frog's skin is smooth and damp, a toad's, dry and very bumpy. A frog's skin dries out easily so the frog needs to stay near ponds or lakes. Dryness doesn't bother toads, so they can stray farther from the water.

Another difference between frogs and toads is their body shape. Toads have squat, chunky bodies and shorter hind legs than frogs. Thus they move more slowly and can't jump as far. Some toads you'll see only at night or if you look in a hole, crevice or burrow. Frogs hop about by day and sing during the evening. They love light and sun, so you'll see many basking on lily pads.

How do chameleons change color?

A chameleon's body is covered with different-colored tiny holes that can be opened or closed by small muscles in the chameleon's skin. When a chameleon wants to hide on a green leaf, it somehow tells some pores to close down so that the red and yellow pigments in the chameleon's skin disappear. That leaves the chameleon looking like part of the leaf. If you watch a chameleon "changing color," you can see that as certain pigments increase or decrease in visibility, it looks as if there's a dye moving through the body. This is not the case. The colors are all there at all times. It's just that some are chosen to be displayed and others are not. A chameleon really knows what it means to "choose your colors."

Why do frogs' necks sometimes look like balloons?

The frogs you see with balloonlike pouches under their chins or sticking out from the sides of their heads are males. All that puffed-up display, plus the loud songs that they sing, are simply to impress the females. Some types of frogs link up with their mate through a "female choice breeding system," which means female frogs choose their favorite singers to mate with. Each male produces its own distinctive call. Keeping its nose and mouth firmly shut, the frog forces air up and down between the mouth and the lungs. Some of this air is forced through the floor of the mouth into an air sac that inflates, and the sound can be heard farther away than a frog can hop in a day. When a lady frog likes what she hears, she swims over to her mate and lets him know that he's the one.

If penguins are birds, why can't they fly?

The penguin is as graceful a flyer as any bird. But it flies not in the air, but in the sea. There it flaps its wings very quickly, just like an air-flying bird, to propel itself through the water. It's so well streamlined that it can even do "dolphin leaps" over and under the water. Penguins stopped air flying many millions of years ago and their wings became rigid, boardlike and too small to support their weight in the air. But they're great paddlers, both underwater and on ice and snow— "tobogganing" is a favorite penguin pastime.

14

Why are penguins black and white?

There are two possible advantages to the penguin's black and white suit. First, it makes the bird very difficult to be seen in the water. A predator looking down from the sky probably can't see the penguin's dark back in the black depths of the sea; and predators swimming below would probably miss the bird's light belly against the sunlight-dappled water.

The second reason is warmth. Since black absorbs heat, black backs help to keep penguins warm. If they're cold, penguins turn their backs to the sun; if they're hot, they face it.

How do penguins keep warm?

A penguin doesn't worry about the cold because it wears four layers of "clothes". Under its thick skin is an even thicker layer of fat, like blubber, which helps to keep heat in its body. And at the base of its oily, tightly-packed, water-proofed feathers are tufts of down that help trap air around the penguin's body. It's a bit like wearing a down jacket, a sweater, thermal underwear and a wet suit.

No matter how long a penguin stays underwater its skin never gets wet. That's because its feathers overlap as tightly as fish scales. There are 22 feathers per dime-sized space on a penguin's skin.

In really cold weather, adult emperor penguins form "huddles" to conserve body heat. Sometimes up to 6,000 penguins stand close together while they incubate their eggs.

15

How do birds know when to start migrating?

Many birds start to head south before the weather gets really cold. But how do they know winter is coming? It's not simply a question of dwindling food supplies. Could it be that they tell the season is about to change by noticing the shortening fall days? Scientists have experimented with wild birds in large cages, gradually shortening the days by turning off electric lights. They discovered that the birds' awareness of the fewer daylight hours caused them to head to the south side of their cage! It was as if they were trying to begin their migration.

And why do birds migrate? The fact that some birds do not migrate gives us an important clue. Birds whose food supplies are not destroyed by cold or covered by snow, such as many woodpeckers or chickadees (which eat larvae or eggs that are on or in tree trunks), needn't migrate because they can find food even during the long winter months. But birds that depend on grain, shoots, insects and other foods that cannot be found in winter have to migrate— or starve.

The tiny ruby-throated hummingbird, for example, travels all the way from Canada to Mexico each winter searching for nectar to drink from flowers. Why doesn't it stay where it's warm all year? Well, one little hummingbird might not need much food, but if all the hummingbirds in North America decided never to leave sunny Mexico, the nectar supply would soon run low. By migrating north again, hummingbirds never run out of food.

Do birds have teeth?

Most birds don't have teeth, but they can still "chew" their food. They swallow little bits of dirt and small stones that rattle around in their gizzard (part of the stomach) and in this way grind up their food. If you feed birds when there's lots of snow on the ground, add crushed egg shells to the bird feed because it might be difficult for birds to find little bits of stone.

Even when a bird is full, it doesn't have to stop eating. At the top of its stomach is a bag called a crop. When the gizzard is full, extra food is stored in the crop. If a bird wants to enjoy a meal in safety and at leisure it will often fill its crop and digest the food later.

When birds migrate, how do they know how to get there?

Birds, it seems, are better navigators than human beings. Scientists still do not fully understand how birds know which direction to head, but it is thought that they use the sun as a compass. To take an accurate bearing from the sun, however, they must also know the time of day since the sun moves to a different place in the sky as the day progresses.

Birds also use stars to find their way on their long flights. But some birds can navigate without any help from either the sun or stars. The homing pigeon is one example. It can fly straight home, even on very cloudy days. How? Scientists think that the earth's magnetic field guides some birds, but they are still trying to find out how.

How can birds fly?

If you have ever held a bird in your hand, you know that it has a very light body. This is because it has hollow bones and air sacs near its lungs. A bird also has very strong wing muscles. Put all these features together and you've got an incredible flying machine. As the bird's wings flap down, the long outer feathers close and push against the air lifting the bird up, while the feathers on the wingtip pull the bird forward. As the bird's wing goes up, the long outer feathers open so that the air can pass between them, while the wingtip feathers push back against the air to keep the bird moving ahead. Birds such as ostriches, of course, don't fly. They tend to have heavy bones, all the better to support their weight as they walk around on land.

Why do birds have feathers?

Bird feathers serve two purposes. First, when fluffed up, feathers trap air that helps to keep the bird warm. Your down-filled jacket works just the same way. Feathers are also essential for flying. Wing feathers help to get the bird up into the air. Tail feathers steer a bird through the sky and keep it balanced on the ground.

Why do birds preen their feathers?

When a bird turns its head around and nuzzles its feathers with its beak, it's said to be preening. You don't have to wait long to see a bird preening its feathers—it does it often, and not just because it wants to look beautiful.

When a bird preens, it takes a beakful of water-repellent oil from a preen gland right above the base of the tail and smooths the oil over its feathers. This makes the feathers waterproof. Feathers that aren't waterproofed get waterlogged, which makes the bird too heavy to fly.

Preening not only oils feathers, it keeps them smooth and removes bugs and dirt. Since dirty feathers let out body heat, unkempt feathers can make flying difficult and feathers that are full of parasites can make a bird sick, preening is a good habit.

Why do birds sing?

Birds sing to attract a mate and to establish their territory. They also chatter to one another. In winter this chattering is quite important. Individual members of a flock of birds—chickadees, for example —give "recognition calls". If a strange bird tries to join the flock or share their feeder but can't give the right call to show it belongs within the flock, the other birds will attack and peck the intruder until it flies away.

How do birds breathe?

Birds need up to 20 times more oxygen when they are flying than when they're resting. They could breathe hard and fast to get enough, but we know they don't. Instead, birds recycle air to get as much oxygen as possible out of each breath and to get rid of the carbon dioxide as quickly as possible. Connected to a bird's lungs are five air sacs. Air that's been through the lungs is stored in these sacs for a fraction of a second, then sent back to the lungs. By recycling each breath in this way, birds squeeze every bit of oxygen they can out of the air they breathe, without wasting energy by breathing twice as fast.

Why don't birds fall off branches when they sleep?

Perching birds have a handy way of staying upright when they settle down to sleep. Because a perching bird has ankles that bend backward and downward, it can clamp its toes tightly around a branch. The bird's weight presses downward, locking the toes and legs in this position. When the bird wants to fly away, it simply straightens its ankles and takes off.

19

How can owls hunt at night?

Perhaps the most amazing thing about an owl is that it could probably hunt blindfolded, zeroing in on its prey by sound alone. Tucked behind its flat face feathers are big, super-sensitive ears that can tune in on the tiniest squeak or rustle. The owl also has excellent eyes, but most hunt at night because that's when prey – mice, rats and moles – come out in search of food.

Do hummingbirds really hum?

Hummingbirds have a very special way of beating their wings – up to 50 times a second in a figure-eight pattern. When you look at a hummingbird in flight all you can see is a blur – but you can hear the wings humming – hence the name.

Why do chickens have white and dark meat?

Dark meat is made up of muscles that have to be stronger than the other muscles in the bird's body because they have so much work to do. Chickens, for example, only have dark meat on their legs, because it's these muscles that are used for walking. Ducks that fly and swim have dark meat all over their bodies because both their chest and leg muscles must work hard. The dark color comes from a special pigment, called myoglobin, that carries oxygen to the muscles for fuel. White meat is made up of muscles that are only used for sudden spurts of energy (for instance, when a chicken flaps its wings). These muscles can get by without so much oxygen. Instead they burn up sugar that's stored in the body. The sugar is used up very quickly, which is why a chicken can't flap for long.

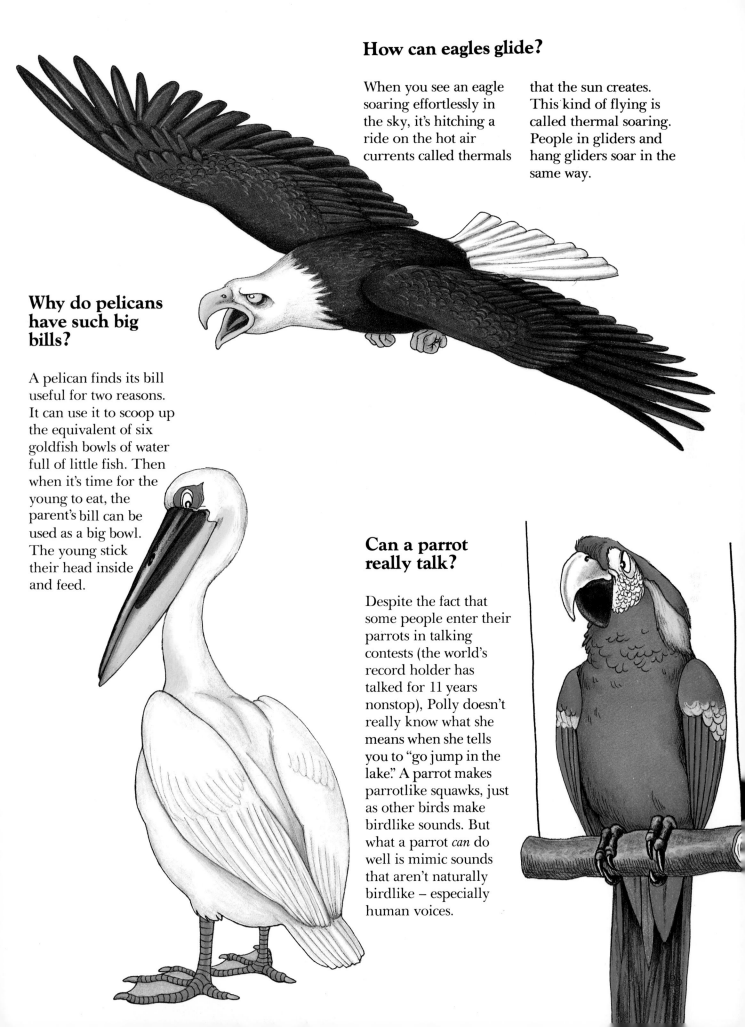

How can eagles glide?

When you see an eagle soaring effortlessly in the sky, it's hitching a ride on the hot air currents called thermals that the sun creates. This kind of flying is called thermal soaring. People in gliders and hang gliders soar in the same way.

Why do pelicans have such big bills?

A pelican finds its bill useful for two reasons. It can use it to scoop up the equivalent of six goldfish bowls of water full of little fish. Then when it's time for the young to eat, the parent's bill can be used as a big bowl. The young stick their head inside and feed.

Can a parrot really talk?

Despite the fact that some people enter their parrots in talking contests (the world's record holder has talked for 11 years nonstop), Polly doesn't really know what she means when she tells you to "go jump in the lake." A parrot makes parrotlike squawks, just as other birds make birdlike sounds. But what a parrot *can* do well is mimic sounds that aren't naturally birdlike – especially human voices.

What's an eggshell made of?

An eggshell is made of layer upon layer of chalklike calcium salts. Because a shell is layered, oxygen and moisture can pass through these layers into the egg, and carbon dioxide and other wastes can escape. Birds that nest near the water must be very careful not to let their eggs fall in. If the eggs sat in water for a long time so much water would pass through the shell that the incubating chicks would drown.

Inside an eggshell is an air space at the larger end. Next is the egg white, called albumen, wrapped in a very thin membrane, which acts as a cushion around the yellow yolk, and the small ovum – the special female reproductive cell – that floats on top of the yolk. The yolk and the ovum don't roll around in the egg because they are held in position by twisted strands of albumen, called the chalaza, that are on either side of the yolk. When birds are incubating their eggs, they will often turn them so that the embryo doesn't stick to the membrane protecting it and become malformed.

22

How long does it take for birds' eggs to hatch?

The time it takes an egg to hatch depends on the species of bird, the egg size and the air temperature. Those birds that spend only a short time in the egg usually will need more parental care when hatched. Baby songbirds, blind, naked and helpless when hatched, are in their eggs for a mere 10 to 14 days.

Chickens, ducks and game birds incubate their eggs for three weeks or longer, so their babies are usually covered with warm down when they hatch. They're usually able to follow their parents almost immediately and to pick up food for themselves. The bird that incubates its eggs the longest is the royal albatross – about 81 days. There are few rules in nature: albatross babies are helpless when they hatch, and they can't fly or hunt for food until they're nearly nine months old.

Why are birds' eggs oval?

There's a very practical reason for certain birds to lay oval eggs. Oval eggs fit well together in a nest and this helps to keep them warm. And even if a nest is no more than a few twigs on a rocky ledge, the eggs will always roll downhill toward the middle.

Different species of birds lay differently shaped eggs. Noddy birds' eggs, for example, are flattened, which helps to keep them from falling off the branches on which they are laid!

Why do some flowers close up at night?

Scientists aren't sure why flowers close at night. Plants that grow straight, such as tulips, probably close at night to protect their delicate inner parts from rain and cold. Whatever the reason, once a flower begins to close at night, it's almost impossible to stop it. The four o'clock flower, for example, shuts up tight late every afternoon and won't open again until early the next morning.

Why do plants lean towards light?

Plants are always moving, although usually they do it so slowly you can't see. Plants move toward sunlight because the more light they get, the more food they can make for themselves and the better they'll grow. To make your plants grow straight, turn their pots a little every day.

Do all plants need sunlight?

About one out of ten plants in the world can get along very well without sunlight. Those that need the sun use it to help them make food. Those that don't need sun feed on other plants or even animals. These plants are called fungi – better known as molds, yeasts and, of course, mushrooms. Food for most mushrooms is rotting plants or animals, so they're part of nature's built-in janitor service.

Why do plants have seeds?

Most, but not all, plants have seeds that are simply baby plants that can eventually grow into big plants. Each seed has two parts: an embryo, which contains a young root that will grow downward to find water and a shoot that will grow up to the light and air; and a storage area, which provides the embryo with food.

Seeds can be so small they look like dust. Or they can be like double coconut seeds, too big to hold in your hand! Most plants that form seeds produce a large number of them because only a few will live. Some seeds die before they find the right spot to grow, others become food for animals.

Why do tree stumps have rings?

For each year of a tree's life you'll see one light and one dark band on the stump, together called an annual ring. Each light-colored ring shows how much the tree has grown each spring and each dark-colored ring shows the late summer and fall growth. By counting the dark rings on a tree stump you can tell exactly how old a tree was when it was cut down. Start counting at the oldest part of the tree: the center.

Trees that have rings are usually found in temperate climates in which plants grow quickly in the spring and early summer and slowly in the late summer and autumn. In the tropics many trees don't have rings. Since it's almost always warm and wet in these areas, trees grow evenly throughout the year.

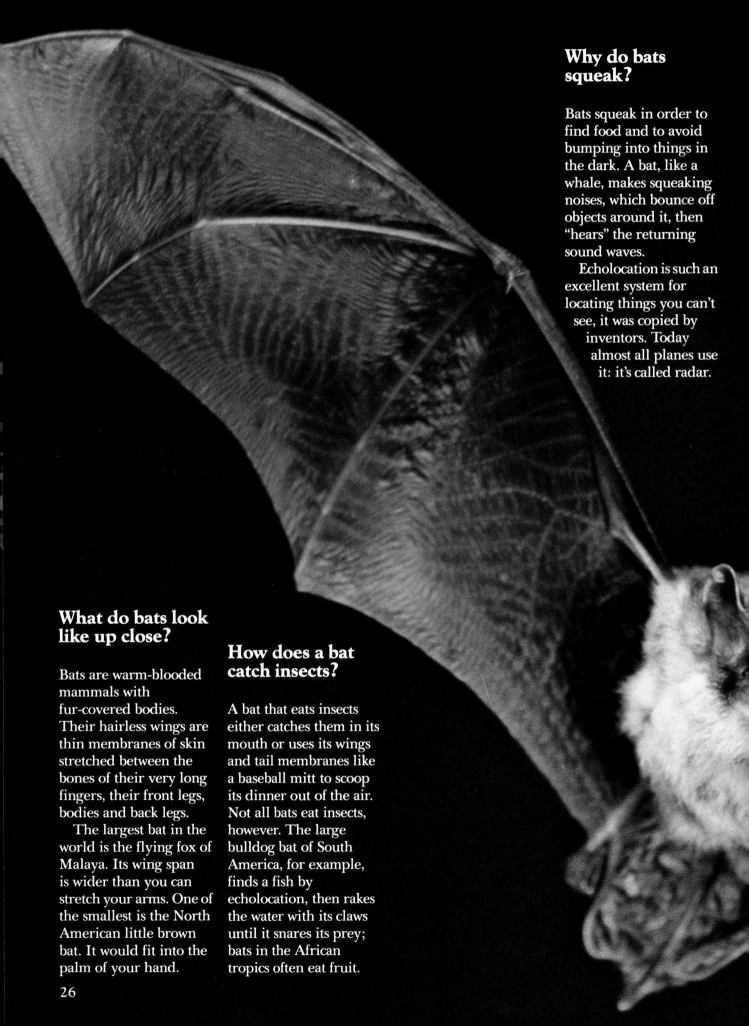

Why do bats squeak?

Bats squeak in order to find food and to avoid bumping into things in the dark. A bat, like a whale, makes squeaking noises, which bounce off objects around it, then "hears" the returning sound waves.

Echolocation is such an excellent system for locating things you can't see, it was copied by inventors. Today almost all planes use it: it's called radar.

What do bats look like up close?

Bats are warm-blooded mammals with fur-covered bodies. Their hairless wings are thin membranes of skin stretched between the bones of their very long fingers, their front legs, bodies and back legs.

The largest bat in the world is the flying fox of Malaya. Its wing span is wider than you can stretch your arms. One of the smallest is the North American little brown bat. It would fit into the palm of your hand.

How does a bat catch insects?

A bat that eats insects either catches them in its mouth or uses its wings and tail membranes like a baseball mitt to scoop its dinner out of the air. Not all bats eat insects, however. The large bulldog bat of South America, for example, finds a fish by echolocation, then rakes the water with its claws until it snares its prey; bats in the African tropics often eat fruit.

What do you do if a bat flies into your home?

Simply open the doors and windows, turn off the lights and stay quiet. Remember, a bat can "see" in the dark because of its echolocation system. Be sure not to touch a bat because its bite can make you very sick. If a bat in your house does not fly away on its own, trap it gently between two objects—a piece of stiff cardboard and a food strainer work well, or even two tennis racquets. Then take it outside and let it go.

Who are a bat's main enemies?

A bat's main enemies are human beings. If a bat eats too many insects that have been sprayed with chemicals, the harmful poisons build up in its body until it grows sick or dies. People who explore caves in winter also run the risk of endangering bats that may be hibernating there. There are records of thousands of frightened bats dying because they used up all their energy trying to escape from their caves.

Are bats blind?

Some people may tell you that bats are so blind they can get entangled in your hair. This is not true. Even though bats have very tiny eyes, which are of little use to them at night, they are very good at finding their way in the dark using echolocation. Only a deaf bat would bump into a person's head.

Do bats lay eggs or have babies?

A female bat gives birth to live babies and nurses them with her milk. She usually has only one baby at a time.

Why do bats hang upside down?

Because a bat burns up energy quickly when it's flying, it must save energy whenever possible. If you've ever grown tired of waiting for a parade you know that standing or even sitting burns up energy. That's because your leg and back muscles have to work against the force of gravity to keep your body upright. So when a bat sleeps or hibernates, it simply hangs upside down by its clawed back feet, like a folded umbrella. Much easier!

Why do so many people hate bats?

Sometimes, unfortunately, people fear things they don't know much about. Bats, for example. But the more you learn about bats, the more you can appreciate them.

What do snakes eat?

Snakes eat all sorts of things. Yellow rat snakes, which live in trees, eat birds, birds' eggs and small mammals they find on the ground. Swamp-dwelling snakes, such as the South American anaconda, snack mostly on fish, but can gobble up a sheep that ventures too close to the water's edge. Some snakes, such as the king snake, even eat poisonous snakes. They can do this because they are immune to other snakes' venom.

Snakes often eat prey larger than themselves. This isn't because their appetites are bigger than their stomachs. Their jaws are held together by an elastic ligament that can stretch and stretch to cover their prey the same way a sock slides over a foot.

When a snake eats an egg, which it loves to do, it first curls around it so that the egg won't roll away. Then the snake opens its jaws and moves the egg into its throat, where sharp spines pierce it and neck muscles squeeze it until it collapses. Once the egg is in its stomach, the snake spits out the empty eggshell. Large snakes, such as constrictors and anacondas, eat pigs in the same way, although they usually will only eat dead pigs. When finished, they spit out the big bones.

Why do snakes shed their skin?

As a snake grows, its skin gets tighter and tighter. To rid itself of its uncomfortably tight girdle, the snake grows a new skin underneath and, when it's ready, slithers out of the old. Younger snakes may shed their skins three or more times a year, whereas older snakes, once they have stopped growing, rarely shed their skins at all.

What is venom? What does it do to people?

There are two kinds of venom, and both are very harmful. One, called neurotoxin, affects a victim's nervous system. Any creatures bitten by cobras or seasnakes get a dose of neurotoxin. This acts on their central nervous system and prevents messages from being sent from their brains to various parts of their bodies. Because their lungs are no longer being told to breathe, the victims die of suffocation.

The other kind of venom, called hemotoxin, works on the bloodstream, causing the blood to coagulate and stop flowing.

Why do snakes stick out their tongues? Do they bite with them?

Forget everything you know about tongues when you think about snakes. A snake isn't being rude when it sticks out its tongue, nor is it licking or tasting. So what good is the tongue? A snake darts its tongue in and out through a hole in its upper jaw to pick up particles in the air to take them to two small cavities in the roof of the snake's mouth. From here, the scent of the particles wafts up to the snake's Jacobson's organ which is above the roof of its mouth. The Jacobson's organ helps the snake know what it is smelling.

What's the longest snake in the world?

Both contenders for the world's longest snake are hard to find. The reticulated python of Southeast Asia, Indonesia and the Philippines has been measured at just over 9.7m/32 feet (they're almost always over 6m/20 feet). And there's a report of a Brazilian anaconda stretching in at more than 11.2m/37 feet. Either one would need six beds lying in a row if it wanted to lie down for a nap!

What is the smallest bug?

You need good eyesight to watch a flea circus. But to watch a circus of hairy-winged beetles and fairy flies performing, you'd also need a very strong magnifying glass. These little insects are much smaller than the period at the end of this sentence.

What's the coldest place on earth?

If you go down to Vostock, Antarctica, take thermal underwear, a down vest, jacket and parka and loads of mittens. The place is usually about −57.8°C/−72°F. In July, the average temperature can drop to −90°C/−130°F.

The hottest place, in case you want to know that too, is Dallol, Ethiopia, near the southern end of the Red Sea. The maximum daily temperature recorded for 10 months of the year is 37.8°C/100°F. It cools down in December and January, though, to an average of 36.7°C/98°F.

What animal weighs the most?

The all-time heavyweight champ is the blue whale. It can weigh more than 16 large elephants, or 1,600 grown men or women.

What's the largest flower?

One Rafflesia arnoldi flower would make a whole bouquet. Its white and orange-brown blossom is about the size of an umbrella and can weigh as much as a fat cat! This Southeast Asian monster flower grows out of the roots of vines on the jungle floor. And just as well, too! Can you imagine the size of plant that would be needed to hold up a flower this big?

What's the biggest bird egg ever laid?

Before it became extinct in the mid-1600s, the elephant bird that lived in Madagascar produced the biggest eggs scientists have ever discovered. These eggs were as big as breadboxes, about two-thirds bigger than those laid by an ostrich. The elephant bird's eggshells were so amazingly strong that they were often used as water jugs once the egg white and yolk had been drained out.

What's the biggest bird?

The average male African ostrich is so tall that he would bump his head walking in your front door. While ostriches may be large, they are not very brave: if they sense danger, they usually choose to run away.

Why does your mouth water when you smell food?

As soon as you smell food, your computerlike brain automatically remembers if it's something you like. It then gets you ready to eat by sending a message to your mouth: "Start the saliva flowing." What's saliva? It's a special fluid that does several important things. It mixes with food to make it easier for you to swallow, and it starts breaking down food and turning it into fuel.

Why and how fast do we blink?

Have you ever tried to outstare someone? It's difficult to do because you've got to force yourself to stop blinking—something you do thousands of times each day without even noticing. If you stopped blinking altogether, you'd probably go blind. That's because the delicate outer covering of your eyeballs would dry out and become infected. Also, blinking washes cleansing tears over your eyeballs to get rid of dust and dirt. So keep on blinking. After all, a blink of the eye takes only 300 milliseconds—much faster than it takes you to think about it!

Why does peeling onions make you cry?

When you peel an onion, a very powerful acid escapes into the air. If some of this acid reaches your eyes, they try to wash it away with tears. How can you avoid crying over an onion? Well, if you don't mind how silly you look, you could wear skin-diving goggles when you're peeling one. Or hold the onion under water as you peel it.

Why do people blush?

Why do people get circles under their eyes when they're tired?

If you could board a tiny boat to travel inside your body, you'd sail along arteries or veins. Your arteries swoosh oxygen-rich, red blood from your heart and lungs to all parts of your body. Your veins sluggishly carry old, used-up, bluish-colored blood back to your heart and lungs, where it is freshened up again. When a person is tired, the entire system that feeds blood into the veins slows down and gets backed up. So what about those dark circles? They're nothing more than old, tired blood lying in the backed-up veins waiting to get back to the heart.

Why do we get butterflies in our stomach?

People blush in threatening situations. These could include when someone makes fun of you or threatens to punch you in the nose. Here's how it all happens. One part of your brain sends a chemical "message" to another part we'll call the "control center" telling it to get your body ready to defend itself. This means more blood will be needed in your muscles. You don't normally notice the extra blood that rushes to, say, your legs or biceps, but you do notice when it reaches your face. It happens automatically, so there's nothing you can do to stop a blush once it starts.

Your stomach is slowly moving all the time to digest or "break down" the food you put into it. When you're nervous, however, your brain directs your stomach to "change gears"—to stop digesting food. It does this to conserve energy so the other muscles in your body will have more energy for whatever action you'll have to take: fighting, fleeing or even reciting a poem in front of the class. Unfortunately, as your stomach changes gears, its smooth movement is disrupted. That's when you feel as if three or four butterflies are flip-flopping around trying to get out.

33

Why do we get dizzy when we spin around?

Chances are when you spin around you get more than dizzy! Try this trick: Turn on the radio or play a record. Stand in the middle of the room, making sure that there are no chairs or tables near by. Close your eyes, cover up one ear and spin yourself around 10 times. Keeping your eyes closed, stop; try to point to the radio or record. Chances are you not only got dizzy, but were fooled as to where the sound was coming from.

Why? When you spin with your eyes closed, you become disoriented. But the problem of losing your balance and locating the sound wrongly also has to do with your ears. Human ears have two kinds of nerves to send messages to the brain. One controls balance, the other controls sound. These nerves are in a liquid base. When you spin, this liquid spins too, and hence the messages that go to your brain get all mixed up, even after spinning for just a moment or two. So your brain continues to receive messages that you're turning even when you're not. Whew!

If you stare at something, why can you sometimes still see it even when you look away?

If you stare hard at, say, a red square for one minute and look quickly away at a white wall or a blank piece of paper, you'll still "see" the square for a few seconds. This happens because you were concentrating so hard on the square that its image became strongly "fixed" in your brain. It keeps remembering the image even after you shifted your eyes. You fooled your brain.

Why do people shrink when they get old?

People don't really "shrink" when they get old. Granny just appears to be getting smaller, and this happens for a variety of reasons. If you slouch, the gristle along your backbone tightens up, which eventually makes it increasingly difficult to stand tall. As you age, your bones tend to become weaker and thinner and this also gives you the appearance of "shrinking."

Why don't some old people remember things?

How your brain remembers things is still baffling physiologists. When you are born, your brain is developing. As you mature, it continues to grow, allowing you to store more and more bits of information there. As you go through life and experience different things, it all gets coded in your brain. An active mind can retrieve these memories easily, although no one is really sure how.

As you grow, your brain keeps growing too, until it reaches its maximum capacity in your late teens. At that time, it's crammed with 10 zillion (10^{12}) neurons where information can be stored. But then thousands of neurons begin to be destroyed every day. And since these neurons are never replaced, your brain's capacity eventually declines.

There's little one can do to stop memory loss from happening, although exercise is important. It keeps blood flowing to the brain.

Why are some horses brown and others spotted?

Horses are different colors for the same reason your hair is either brown, black, red or blond. Color is inherited. Because most people prefer solid-colored horses, these tend to be bred more often. In some areas, such as the North American midwest, however, leopard – marked Appaloosas are the favorites, so you'll probably see more there.

How fast can horses run?

Very quickly! Over a short distance, quarter horses, bred for sprinting, would win the race, running about 18 m/60 feet per second. Thoroughbreds, high-spirited, streamlined horses whose ancestors are from Arabia, will run on the average 17 m/56 feet per second for three-quarters to 1½ miles.

Do horses like to race?

Horses like to run, but probably wouldn't choose to cover the distances we force them to. Because horses have a very competitive instinct, they resent being passed by other horses, and it's this that makes them try to stay ahead of the others during a race.

Why do wild horses live in herds?

Horses live in groups for protection and, some scientists believe, for companionship. A typical herd is made up of a stallion, several mares and several immature horses. In the North American west, groups of several hundred horses sometimes band together, but the average herd ranges in size from five to 40 horses.

How can you tell a wild horse from a domesticated horse?

The only true wild horses still around today are pony-like horses that stand about 127 cm/50 inches high. These Przewalskis, originally from the area around the China/Mongolia border in central Asia, now mostly live on game farms and in zoological parks. You'd know one if you saw it, not only by its size but also by its short mane, dull coloring and stocky body. Many North American horses that run free are called "wild," but they are really domesticated ones that escaped long ago as the settlers and pioneers forged across the continent.

37

How long does it take a horse to have babies?

A mare carries her foal for almost a year: 330 days. That might seem like a long time, but when the horse is finally born it's so well developed it can usually stand up within an hour or two of birth. Which is a good thing, because it needs to stand to reach its mother's underbelly for milk. Once a colt has had some milk and tested its legs – most often five or six hours after birth – it's ready to run with the herd. This was important in the wild, when herds had to keep on the move to find food and avoid predators.

How much does a horse eat?

Just to maintain itself, the average horse eats the equivalent of 35 to 40 large salad bowls full of dry hay a day. A working horse could probably pack away double that amount. Because a horse's stomach isn't big, and because it takes a lot of hay to give a horse all the nourishment it needs, horses must also eat corn, oats, barley and soybean meal for energy and protein.

How can horses sleep standing up?

Once a horse is two or three years old you'll rarely find it lying down to nap. You couldn't sleep standing up because you collapse when you are relaxed, but horses are able to lock their legs so as to stay upright. Horses sleep very little and very lightly and can rest without actually sleeping. Some horses never lie down, some do. Occasionally old horses' spines get a bit stiff, which makes it even more difficult for them to lie down and get up.

Why do horses wear shoes?

A horse's hoof is a big wraparound toenail that is tough enough for running on the ground but needs protection for traveling over roads. Horses, therefore, have their hooves trimmed regularly, and are fitted with iron shoes that are nailed in place. A horse that does a lot of work needs new shoes every six weeks or so! Being shod doesn't hurt because the shoes are nailed onto the non-living part of the horse's hooves, a part that is much like the white ends of your fingernails.

What's horse sense?

Horses seem to be able to sense problems, things that are unusual or wrong. We say people have horse sense if they can sense when "all is not well." Horse sense, for horses, is an instinct left over from their wild days. Horses are better built for escaping than fighting, so they needed to be able to sense trouble in time to avoid walking right into it.

Why do horses have tails?

A horse finds its tail pretty handy. On those days in summer when insects buzz around a horse's ears and back, the tail is an excellent fly swatter. You can often see horses standing in pairs, head to tail, swishing their tails over their own and a companion's back and head. That way they get twice the protection with half the effort.

A horse also uses its tail to show how it's feeling. A happy horse can often be seen with its tail up and over its back. If a horse is feeling out of sorts it "wrings" its tail, swishing it back and forth and around in a circle, just as people wring their hands when they're anxious.

Is a duck-billed platypus a duck or a mammal?

A duck-billed platypus (also called a duckbill, watermole or duckmole) has hair and feeds its babies milk and is therefore classified as a mammal. But a platypus is a most unusual mammal: it lays eggs and the male can squirt venom from its hind ankles for defense and to subdue a female during mating.

The platypus, while not a duck, is quite ducklike. It has a wide, rubbery bill, just right for rooting out the crayfish, shrimps, worms, mollusks and other small water animals that it dearly loves to eat. Also, like a duck, the platypus lives both in water and on land. Its webbed feet help it swim easily and its hind feet serve as rudders. On land it pulls back the webbing on its forefeet so it can burrow and claw easily.

Where do platypuses live?

You can find platypuses in fresh-water streams and lakes in southeastern Australia and Tasmania. They live in long (4.5-9 m/15-30 foot) burrows that feature one entrance on land and one in the water, and, for defense, mud and earth blockades built at intervals between the two entrances.

One end of a platypus's burrow is a nesting chamber lined with wet grass and leaves carried there by the female on her tail. The female lays one to three somewhat leathery eggs, which take about 10 to 12 days to hatch. The female rarely leaves her chamber while caring for her eggs, but when she does she rebuilds the blockades – rather like you locking the door when you go out.

How does a platypus feed its young?

Unlike other mammals, a female platypus has no teats. Her babies lap up milk that flows from milk-producing slits in her abdomen. Young platypuses are born hairless and blind and their eyes don't open for nearly 11 weeks. When born, platypuses have teeth, but these are later replaced by horny ridges that become a bill. Babies are weaned at four months and become mature at about 2½ years. All in all, platypuses live about ten years.

How can a platypus see underwater?

When a platypus dives underwater, its eyes and the inner ears, which are in a furrow on either side of its head, are closed. This means that the platypus is blind and deaf when underwater. But that doesn't really matter, because it relies on its bill to root out its food.

What kind of fish are jellyfish?

Jellyfish, despite their name, aren't really fish at all. They have no fins, scales or bones, not even a head. Some people think they look like a floating bag of jelly, others suggest an umbrella with streamers. But a jellyfish is simply an unusual animal made up of two layers of cells with water in between. Cells in different parts of the jellyfish have different tasks to perform. Some cells sting prey, others catch it, some digest it, others lay eggs.

What is a seashell?

A seashell is the hard, protective covering for soft-bodied animals such as oysters or clams. Clams, oysters and scallops have two shells (either side by side, or top and bottom) that open and shut. Garden snails and conches have only one shell to peek out of from time to time. Most shells are made up of three layers: an outside armor; a middle layer that gives the shell its strength and color; and an inner layer that's so smooth it is pleasant for the shell's owner to be next to.

Is a seahorse a fish?

A seahorse is a fish, but a very peculiar one. It swims upright, using the fin on its back to push it along, and has a very nimble tail that can be wrapped around seaweed almost as a monkey wraps its tail around a branch. Even a seahorse's eyes are unusual. Each is on a turret and can move independently. But the most unusual thing about seahorses is that the males look after the eggs. The mother lays up to 200 eggs in a pouch on the male's belly. He fertilizes the eggs and keeps them safe until they hatch (about four or five weeks later). Then the tiny, perfectly formed baby seahorses swim away.

Do electric eels really give off shocks? How?

Adult electric eels use their electric power to kill prey and defend themselves. They also use their electrical power like radar to "see" through murky waters, which is important because eels are virtually blind by the time they are adults.

How does it all work? Inside an eel's tail are three "batteries," one large and two small, made up of muscle and nerve endings. An eel is constantly "sensing" the water around it. The sensitivity of this electric field around the eel lets it know if something nearby is a rock, a log, or a live or dead fish. When an eel senses something swimming nearby, it sends an extra electric impulse from the large "battery" through the water. This impulse bounces back so the eel can calculate how far away the object is. Unfortunately for the object, this impulse can also kill it. A full-grown electric eel can produce enough electricity to light up as many as 10 40-watt light bulbs – probably as many as you have in your house right now.

How do oysters make pearls?

An oyster, like most mollusks, lives inside a shell lined with a smooth substance. That substance, in an oyster, is called mother of pearl and it's especially smooth. Sometimes, something such as a grain of sand will get inside the oyster's shell; when this happens, the oyster surrounds the grit spot with layers of shell material to prevent its tender body from being scratched. So that's all a pearl is: "dirt" covered with enough perfectly smooth layers of mother of pearl to make a tiny ball.

Where is a starfish's head?

Believe it or not, a starfish gets along very well without a head. Instead it has special cells all over its back that are sensitive to tastes and smells; a small, red spot on the tip of each arm that can "see" changes of light and shade; and a tiny slit in the middle of its underside, which it uses for a "mouth."

A starfish eats almost anything it encounters, including oysters, shrimps or barnacles. One meal will sometimes take as long as three days to finish. Even shells don't keep a starfish away from a meal. When a starfish finds a tasty shellfish, such as a clam, it simply wraps its arms around it, holds on tight and pulls. The clam uses its own muscles to keep its shell tightly shut, but eventually those muscles tire. When they relax, the starfish opens up the clam's shell, moves its stomach into the shell and begins to eat.

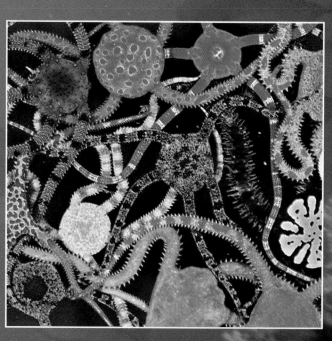

Why do fish swim in schools?

Scientists aren't completely sure why some fish swim in schools. But they do know that there is never a leader or a "teacher" and that some fish schools are very small, having as few as three members—while others can have as many as 1,000 fish.

It is believed that fish swim in schools for protection. The larger the school, the less chance any one individual has of being eaten. If a fish school is threatened, its members often move closer together as if trying to hide behind one another. And it works. The big fish attacking gets confused by the crowd of little fish swimming this way and that. It's like trying to play tennis with several balls at the same time.

Schools of fish have developed several other group tactics for darting away from predators. If a big fish sneaks up from behind, the school might split into two groups, turn and swim around behind it, then regroup again. That leaves the predator wondering where his prey went. If a big fish attacks from the side, the little fish scatter in all directions, which also confuses the predator. It all proves that, for fish, there's definitely safety in numbers.

Do fish sleep?

Most fish spend part of each 24-hour period "asleep." Being asleep to a fish, however, can mean anything from simply slowing down all movement while still being aware of what's going on around, to losing consciousness completely, as humans do when they sleep. Open-water fish, such as herring or tuna, hang motionless in the water at night. Some fresh-water fish, such as catfish, find a log or river bank to shelter under during the day. Other fresh-water fish, such as perch, often hide under overhanging rocks during the night. Still others, such as rockfish and grouper, don't appear to sleep at all, but instead rest against rocks, bracing themselves with their fins. And in case you're wondering, fish don't close their eyes to sleep. They can't. They don't have eyelids.

How do fish stop in water?

A fish uses its dorsal fin for stability, rather like the keel on a boat, to keep it from rolling over; its pelvic and pectoral fins for steering; and its tail fin to propel itself along. When a fish wants to slow down or stop, it spreads out its two pairs of pelvic and pectoral fins almost like a parachute dragging in the water. Then it relaxes and coasts to a stop.

Why do fish jump?

There are several reasons why a fish jumps. Sometimes it jumps to dislodge a hook from its mouth, other times to escape a predator or to shake off parasites. A fish also jumps to catch insects that skim the top of the water, especially in the evening when the water is calm. Some fish, such as salmon, have become famous for their jumps up large waterfalls on their way to their spawning grounds. Many scientists also agree that fish sometimes jump for no apparent reason.

Can fish hear?

Fish hear in different ways. A few fish *feel* sound vibrations, just as we feel bass notes on a sound system, but most don't have eardrums like ours. Instead, they hear through their sides, where they have a line of pores called the "lateral line." These pores respond to pressure changes just as our eardrums do. The pores sense any movement in the water so, for example, fish know if a person or another fish is swimming nearby.

Some fish, the catfish, the midshipman and the Atlantic cod, for example, have inner ears as well. These fish tend to make buzzing or purring noises during courtship or when they are staking out their territory, guarding their eggs or in danger. Scientists believe that a fish that makes noise can hear it.

What are fish scales?

A typical fish body is covered with thin, bony scales that overlap like roof shingles to protect a fish's skin. As a fish grows, its scales increase in size and lost scales are replaced. You can often tell how old a fish is by counting the growth ridges on its scales.

Scales are different depending on the fish. Some fish, such as the turbot, have very small, delicate scales, while the tarpon which lives in the ocean and the Australian lungfish have scales that are bigger than the size of a quarter. A few fish, such as catfish, have no scales at all.

How many insects are there?

At the moment this is being written, almost 800,000 species of insects have been catalogued. But by the time you read this, that figure will be wrong, because every year scientists are finding thousands of new species. Approximately 75 to 80 percent of the animal kingdom is made up of insects (there are almost 300,000 species of beetle alone), and they've been around a long time. Insects' origins can be traced back 350 million years – which means insects were old by the time dinosaurs appeared on earth years later.

How many kinds of monkeys are there?

There are almost 200 species of primates in the world including monkeys, and related apes and prosimians (animals such as Lemurs). Almost all monkeys live in warm climates except for a few, like the Japanese macaques, who keep from being chilly by lounging around in hot springs.

How fast do insects fly?

There are hundreds of thousands of different kinds of insects and they all cruise at different speeds.

If you are keen to organize an insect's Olympic team, make sure you include dragonflies. They'll whiz to the finish line at 30 kmph/18.7 mph, far ahead of the 3.2 kmph/2 mph mosquito, the 6.4 kmph/4 mph housefly or the 19 kmph/12 mph butterfly or wasp.

The fastest cruising insect ever reported is the deer botfly, a tropical insect that flies at 40 kmph/25 mph. When trying to avoid an enemy, most insects can put on a spurt. If it's threatened, a dragonfly can double its speed but not for long.

How old is the oldest living tree?

California is home to the world's oldest living single tree, a 4,600-year-old bristling pine. There was another bristlecone 300 years older, but it was cut down in 1964. Both of those trees were alive when the pyramids of Egypt were being built and scientists think that the one that is still standing could live 1,000 years longer.

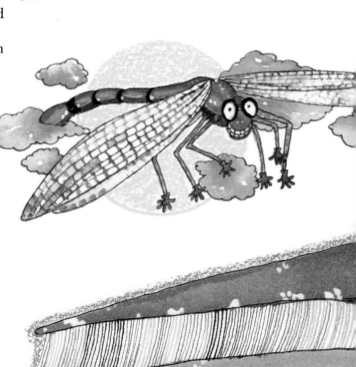

What's the fastest fish?

Don't ever try to race a sailfish – it can swim more than 96 kmph/60 mph – that's as fast as many a highway speed limit.

What's the heaviest bird that flies?

If you've ever tried to get aloft by flapping your arms, you'll be able to imagine what the Kori bustard of East Africa has to do to fly. It weighs about as much as a nine-year-old human, so perhaps it's no surprise that even though it has wings twice as long as your arms, it only manages to get as high as 60-91 m/ 200-300 feet above the ground.

How many kinds of birds are there?

There are more than 8,600 species of birds. Some birds, such as the barnswallow, have many relatives around the world within their species, while others, such as the kiwi, have just a few in one area. There are tens of millions of individual birds that live on earth today and they all have two things in common: they all lay eggs and they all have feathers.

What's the biggest turtle in the world?

Turtles that live in the sea are the largest and heaviest. Imagine paddling into a leatherback. Its flippers span 3.6 m/12 feet, it has a shell bigger than an average kitchen table and it weighs almost as much as a subcompact car.

What's the biggest animal on earth?

The blue whale, as long as two buses end to end, is the biggest animal on earth and a good bet for the animal with the largest lungs too. Imagine what would happen if blue whales could sneeze!

Why do walruses turn pink?

A lone walrus is an unhappy walrus. Walruses love to be close together, even though it makes for a lot of arguments. When the walruses are snuggly and warm, the blood vessels in their blubber open up and blood rushes to their skin, which is why they turn pink.

Why do pigs wallow in the mud?

Pigs don't perspire much so they wallow in mud to cool down on a hot day. First they lie on one side, then on the other, so that even their eyes and ears are covered with mud. Mud not only protects their skin from nasty pests, but also from sunburn.

Do whales spout water?

The spray you see coming from a whale's blowhole is a big breath of hot, moist air, which turns into a cloud as it cools. Mixed with that air is salt water that was trapped in a trough rimming the whale's blowhole.

Do all animals sleep?

All creatures sleep in their own way, although not necessarily the way you do. For example, horses and elephants can sleep standing up. Snakes sleep with their eyes open (because they have no eyelids) and some insects sleep by simply slowing down their body processes for a while. People once believed that sharks couldn't ever stop to sleep because they had to keep swimming in order to force water through their gills to breathe and keep afloat. Recent studies have shown that this is not necessarily true. Some sharks have been found "sleeping" on the bottom of caves along the Mexican coast.

Why do some animals have eyes in the sides of their head and others have them in front?

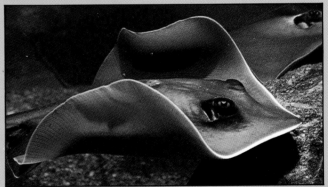

Having eyes in the sides of your head is the next best thing to having eyes in the back of your head – especially if you're a defenseless animal. With eyes on the side you can see predators trying to sneak up on you. Predators, on the other hand, are better off with eyes that face forward. To be able to judge distances, both eyes need to focus on the same object at once.

How long can a camel last without water?

A camel can run nonstop across a desert for 18 hours each day, carrying the equivalent weight of eight heavy suitcases on its back. And it can do this for over 30 days without eating or drinking. One Australian dromedary is reported to have gone for 37 days without even so much as a sip!

Why do some camels have one hump and others two?

No one really knows the answer to this question, although some scientists think it might have something to do with where camels live.

There are two main types of camels: dromedaries, which have one hump, and bactrians, which have two. The one-humped dromedary, which is the one you've probably seen in desert movies, lives in the hot, sandy countries of North Africa, the southeastern Mediterranean region, India and Australia. The two-humped bactrian lives in the deserts of Mongolia, where it gets very cold each winter. Scientists wonder if its second hump developed to store extra fat for winter.

What's the difference between caribou and reindeer?

Caribou live in Canada and reindeer live in Europe and Asia, but they both belong to the same species and are relatives of the deer family. Their noses are never red like Rudolph's, but they are furry to keep the reindeer warm.

Why do dogs pant?

Don't hush up your dog if it's panting – it's just trying to cool off. Humans get cool from the outside of their bodies by perspiring, but dogs, and other furry animals that don't sweat much, cool off from the inside by panting. Moving air quickly in and out of their lungs helps them to get rid of heat inside.

Why is a cat's tongue so rough?

A lick from a tabby is like being rubbed by sandpaper, but the flick of a tiger's tongue could tear your skin. All cats have comblike spikes called papillae on their tongues that they use for brushing their fur and scraping meat from bones. When they drink, the cat's papillae trap liquid on the tongue. The larger the cat, the larger and rougher the papillae.

Why do cats turn their ears around?

Cup your hands behind your ears and you'll understand better why cats can hear so well. But it's not only the funnel shape of a cat's ears that helps it to pick up sound. Every cat has up to 20 muscles in each ear so it can swivel them in almost any direction. Watch a cat do this while hunting. It's listening to every squeak and rustle, including some you can't hear at all.

Why does a cat's fur stand on end?

A cat's fur, consisting of large guard hairs and shorter underfur, protects its body from bites, scratches and hot and cold temperatures. Each guard hair is attached to a muscle that makes it stand on end whenever the cat is angry or alarmed. And because this is so startling to see, it is a very good scare tactic indeed.

Why do cats have whiskers?

The stiff, wiry whiskers sticking out over a cat's eyes and from the sides of its face, are sensitive feelers. Even the slightest touch on these whiskers sends a message to the cat's brain. Thus a cat knows that if it can squeeze its head through a narrow opening without its whiskers being touched, the rest of its body will probably be able to get through too.

How do cats purr?

Scientists know that most cats purr when they're happy, and that mother cats purr to call their newborn kittens at feeding time. Cats also purr when they're getting a lot of attention, which is probably why your cat may purr on the vet's examination table. But, alas, scientists aren't really sure *how* cats purr.

One theory is that the purring noise is caused by blood rushing through a large, funnel-shaped vein in the cat's chest. When a cat is happy, extra blood flows through this vein, causing it to vibrate where it narrows to pass through the cat's liver and diaphragm. The diaphragm is a muscle stretched tight like a drumskin so it amplifies the vibrations into a low, rumbling sound—purring.

Why does a skunk make such a horrible smell?

Why do rabbits hop?

A rabbit has such long, strong hind legs and short front legs that hopping is the fastest and most efficient way to travel. A full-grown white-tailed jack rabbit can hop 64 km/ph/40 miles per hour.

How many kinds of animals are there in the world?

There are more than one million kinds of animals that have been identified and scientists are finding many more every year.

A skunk is small—about the size of a large house cat— can't climb very well and doesn't run fast. It hasn't needed to learn how to fight back successfully or even how to escape from a predator. Instead, it makes its enemies run away by squirting a foul-smelling liquid called mercaptan.

A skunk doesn't have to spray its enemies very often because they recognize its bold stripes that warn, "Stay away or I'll spray." It's just as well, because a skunk can only make enough mercaptan to spray five times a week.

Why do dogs' ears prick up when people don't even notice a noise?

Dogs make up for their ho-hum sight with a super sense of hearing. They can hear a noise a block away that a person wouldn't hear if it were right next door. Rover hears almost twice as well as you and about a third better than most cats.

Do furry animals get hot in the summer?

Don't feel sorry for your shaggy dog on a hot day. If you stick your hands into its fur, you'll find that the hair close to the skin is much cooler than that at the surface. Sheep beat the heat exactly the same way, but their fleece is one of nature's best insulators. The wool next to their skin can be 5°C/11°F cooler than the wool at the surface.

What's the difference between a donkey and a mule?

You might say a donkey is an ass—a domesticated wild ass. It's related to a horse, but has long ears, a large head, a short mane, a tuft of hair on the end of the tail as well as two dark bands on the back and the shoulders.

A mule is the offspring of a female horse and a male donkey. Mules are usually larger, stronger and less nervous than donkeys.

Where did the expression "playing possum" come from?

Even though most people have never seen an opossum, almost everyone knows how to "play possum"—it means not moving, hoping you'll be left alone. And that's exactly what the opossum does when being hunted by its enemies, such as an owl, bobcat or hawk. Curled up on its side with its eyes and mouth open, the opossum looks so lifeless that its enemies soon lose interest, or perhaps lose sight of their prey, and move off in search of a more appetizing dinner. A few minutes later the opossum looks quickly around, gets up and ambles off as if nothing happened.

Although it might seem to be awfully clever of the opossum to pretend to be dead in order to fool its enemies, it is believed that "playing dead" is simply an automatic reaction probably brought on by fear. If it does not play dead it usually defends itself with its teeth.

Do polar bears hibernate?

Only a pregnant polar bear dens up for winter. The temperature inside her snug snow den is about 21°C/70°F warmer than the air outside. She sleeps a lot, but gets up from time to time to adjust the temperature in her ice cave by poking a hole in the roof or closing it up with snow. All polar bears, other than mothers and babies, are loners, wandering summer and winter in search of food, seeking shelter during the most terrible storms. Males and females are together only at mating time, so fathers never see their babies.

How do you taste things?

Tasting chocolate, lemon, potato chips or anything else puts not only your tongue to work, but also your nose and eyes.

If you don't believe that you need your eyes, nose and tongue to taste, try this trick on some friends: Cut equal-sized pieces of raw peeled potato, apple and radish. Blindfold your friends and ask them to hold their noses. Then have them taste the potato, the apple and the radish. They won't know which food is which.

Why? Because there wasn't enough information for their brains to tell them what they were eating. Anyone who has ever had a cold knows this too. When you're all stuffed up, food doesn't have any taste.

What happens when you sneeze?

Sneezing protects your lungs. When dust sneaks past the cleaning system in your nose and throat, an alarm goes off in your brain. The tubes leading to your lungs quickly narrow so that the dust "invader" can't squeeze through them. Of course, when you try to breathe out, you can't because your tubes are no longer wide enough. Soon the pressure becomes too great and—achoo—your tubes are blasted open by an explosion of air traveling as fast as a World Series' pitch!

Why doesn't it tickle when you tickle yourself?

When someone else tickles you, a fast message is sent from your skin to your brain. Your brain quickly makes you react—you laugh, or scream and pull away. If you tickle yourself, your brain does not bother to make you respond because it knows that it's in control of the tickler.

What are goose bumps?

When the skin on your arms and legs looks like the bumpy skin of a freshly plucked goose, you'll know that your brain is trying to warm you up. At the base of the thousands of little hairs that cover your body are tiny muscles. When these muscles tense, they make your hair stand on end. This traps a layer of air close to your skin, where it can be warmed by your body. The bumps you see are the little muscles straining to hold up each hair. It's easy to see why you get goose bumps when you're cold, but what about when you're scared? Your brain is warming up your muscles in case you need to fight or run away.

Where do tears come from?

Behind your eyelids, at the outer edge of your eyes, are small glands called lacrimal glands. They are continuously at work, making fluid to squirt into your eyes, keeping them moist and clean. When you cry, these glands work overtime so tears flow out drainage holes into your nose, making you sniffle. Your nose isn't running—your glands are dripping.

Why does skin shrivel up when you stay in bath water too long?

You get "prune fingers" and even "prune feet" when your skin dries out. It might seem odd to you that your skin can become dry and wrinkly when you're sitting up to your neck in bath water, but it works like this. Soapy water, especially, robs your skin of its protective coating of oil. This allows water inside your skin to slowly ooze out into the bath water, so your skin is actually drying from the inside out. When your skin has lost too much water, some of its cells collapse, forming wrinkles.

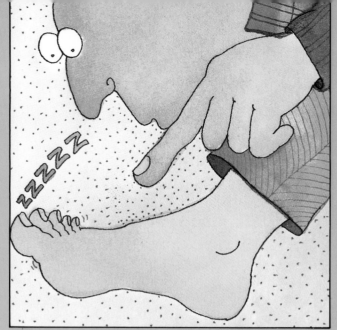

Why does your foot fall asleep when you sit for too long?

Remaining in one position for a long time can prevent your blood from circulating. For example, sometimes a blood vessel is pinched closed when you sit cross-legged. This cuts off the supply of blood to your leg and foot, making muscles and nerves there feel numb. When you get up or shake a foot that's "asleep," you get a tingly feeling because the blood starts to flow again, "waking up" the nerves and muscles.

Why do people yawn?

Suppose you're in a boring class and you start to nod off. All of a sudden – yawn! It seems a silly thing to do, and, indeed, scientists don't really know what causes yawns or what effect they have.

Yawning may be your body's way of taking in a quick "oxygen snack" when you are tired and your brain needs some oxygen in a hurry. Unfortunately, this snack doesn't last long; you may be fast asleep before the class is over.

What is a hiccup?

Since it's hard to get hiccups to happen in a lab, scientists aren't completely sure what they are. Some believe that the problem is caused by the glottis which is a piece of flesh at the top of your voice box that flaps up and down. Designed to keep things such as water, saliva and food from sliding down into your windpipe, the movement of the glottis is supposed to keep rhythm with your breathing. Sometimes, though, the glottis gets out of rhythm and this, they think, is what gives you hiccups. Why the glottis gets out of rhythm has scientists baffled. Some believe it's caused by a small problem in the control center of the brain – when the brain skips a beat it causes your glottis to get out of rhythm too.

What is a sixth sense?

Have you and a friend had exactly the same thought at the same moment? Some people think it's your sixth sense at work. Most of our information about the world comes from our five senses: sight, hearing, touch, taste and smell. Those who believe we also have a sixth sense claim that this special sense allows us to read minds, "look" into the future and even dream things before they happen. Many scientists aren't convinced that we really have a sixth sense. They think it's just coincidence rather than some mysterious mental power at work. But many others believe that people aren't able to understand how we respond to certain kinds of extrasensory or "psychic" information and that therefore it is best to remain open minded about the possibility of a "sixth sense."

Why do people snore?

When people sleep some of their nose and throat muscles relax and droop slightly. Sometimes they block the airways from the lungs and create turbulent whirlpools of air, which behave sort of like air in a pipe organ. When people snore, what you hear is this turbulent air flow and, sometimes, the sound of the throat muscles gently flapping as well.

What makes the sound when you snap your fingers?

As you snap your fingers, your middle finger suddenly slips off your thumb and, a split second later, strikes the fleshy pad at the base of your thumb. The snap is caused by skin hitting skin and by air erupting out from between your finger and thumb. These sudden motions send tiny molecules of air crashing into one another. This sets up a chain reaction of molecule collisions – a bit like dominoes falling down in a row. When the air molecules in your ear crash against your ear drums, your brain hears the collision as a "*snap*."

Why do people get cranky?

Your body is an amazing machine – and, like all machines, it needs regular maintenance. Every time you go to sleep, it's as if thousands of tiny mechanics leap into action all over your body, mending worn tissues, fixing the frayed connections between nerve endings, and more – all to get you ready for the next day. When you feel tired, your body is telling you, "C'mon, it's time for some maintenance, please." To make certain that you've understood the message – and that everyone else understands too – your brain makes you feel short tempered and cross. So when your mom says, "Go to bed, you're cranky," she's got your message.

Why do some people go bald?

Alas, there isn't a very satisfactory answer to this question. Some scientists believe you inherit baldness from your parents. Others believe some people's changing body chemistry causes them to go bald, while still others think that if your blood circulation is poor, and thus your scalp doesn't get enough nourishment, your hair falls out. Sometimes loss of hair is simply caused by poor hair care. One fact is certain: Men are much more likely to go bald than women.

How can a fly walk upside-down on the ceiling and not fall off?

Look at this fly's middle foot. It's wide and has two big hooks and soft, rounded pads. Now imagine you're this fly. You weigh practically nothing at all, so you're like an astronaut in space. Because gravity isn't pulling you down and you have six hooked feet that can grab all the craters and cracks in the ceiling, you are well anchored up there.

What are fireflies and how do they glow in the dark?

Fireflies are not flies at all. During the day the firefly is a dull, not very pretty, slow-moving beetle. But by night, that same beetle glows. Male fireflies flash on and off to signal to females that they're looking for a mate. Some females flash their lights to attract males – both to mate with and eat! Amazingly, although there are more than 100 different types of fireflies in North America, each type has its own special "Morse code." This means that a female never makes the mistake of eating a male from her own group. How does a firefly make light? Chemicals in a special "light organ" below its abdomen combine with oxygen that the firefly breathes in.

Where do flies go in the winter?

Flies spend the winter in a variety of ways, depending on the type. The average adult housefly often sleeps through winter in a building. You may notice flies falling from the rafters in your school gym in February or March. These flies have spent the winter there, hidden away from the cold, but as spring begins to warm things up they become more active. When you haven't eaten for a long time, you sometimes feel groggy, which is just how the flies feel when they wake up.

Other flies spend the winter as eggs laid in garbage or in the rotting carcasses of animals or other insects. These eggs remain safe and warm over the winter and begin to hatch in spring. Still other flies hatch maggotlike larval forms and spend the winter burrowing in soil, plant tissue or garbage until they change into adult flies when the air begins to warm up in spring.

What are an insect's wings made of?

Most insects have two pairs of wings—a forewing and a hindwing—on each side of their body. (Some have only one pair of wings and others are wingless.) Insect wings are usually membranous, which means they are very thin, almost transparent, like cellophane. Some wings look thick and leathery, others are hairy and still others are scalelike, but underneath them all you'll usually discover the same membranous material.

Wings are made up of veins and cells (a cell being the empty space between the veins). When an insect hatches, it immediately pumps blood into the veins in its wings. When this happens, the wings expand almost like balloons to their full adult size.

Why do moths like light?

No one really knows why moths are attracted by electric or ultraviolet light. Some scientists believe this is because moths use moonlight to guide themselves at night. A porch light confuses them and because they are confused, they fly around in circles.

Flying around artificial lights at night is a dangerous thing for moths to do because it makes it easy for such enemies as bats and toads to spot them.

Many moths aren't attracted to light at all. And for some reason, females seldom come near an electric light until after they've laid their eggs.

What's the difference between moth and butterfly caterpillars?

Both moth and butterfly caterpillars begin as tiny eggs laid by their mothers on a leaf. When the eggs hatch into caterpillars, you can hardly tell the difference.

Both moth and butterfly caterpillars feed on the leaves of trees and grow and grow. As they do, they shed their skin several times. Each time this happens a creature wriggles out that still looks like a caterpillar.

After five sheddings, or molts, the last larval skin comes off and the caterpillars go into a new stage of their life: the pupal stage. Now differences begin to appear. Both moth and butterfly caterpillars spin out a small ball of silk from a special gland in their bodies, and use this ball to attach their hind end to a leaf or plant stem.

A butterfly caterpillar may also spin a line of silk around the middle of its body to anchor it more securely in place.

The moth caterpillar usually then spins enough silk to completely surround its body. Once it's covered in this light, strong silk ball, the moth caterpillar is said to be in a cocoon.

Most butterfly caterpillars don't spin cocoons, but they too are protected from the wind, cold and enemies. Beneath the butterfly caterpillar's last molt is a hard chrysalis case.

Both the chrysalis and the cocoon seem to hang there quietly, but inside a great drama is happening. Within weeks, months or over the winter (depending on the species), the caterpillar changes form. What breaks out will be an adult butterfly or moth.

How can you tell the difference between a moth and a butterfly?

Moths tend to hide by day and fly by night. Seeing them in the daytime is often difficult because they are well camouflaged so birds can't find them as they rest on tree trunks or leaves. But if you do find one, you'll probably discover it has a thick, hairy body and often feathery, fernlike antennae.

Butterflies, which do fly during the day, are not generally as hairy or woolly as moths and tend to be more brightly colored. At the tips of their long, slim feelers or antennae, butterflies often have little decorative knobs.

If you're still not certain whether you're seeing a butterfly or a moth, look at the way it rests. Generally a moth will sit with its wings laid out flat while a butterfly will fold its wings up over its back.

Why do most people itch after being bitten by a mosquito?

If you itch after being bitten by a mosquito, it's because you're allergic to a chemical the mosquito injects into you with its saliva to keep your blood from clotting. Depending on how sensitive you are, this chemical, called histamine, can cause the swelling and itching to last for days.

No one knows why some people attract more mosquitoes than others, but here are a couple of tricks that may help to reduce your chances of a bite. Because mosquitoes appear to be attracted by dark colors and rough textures, wear pale yellow or white. A smooth textured, pale outfit will be much less attractive to a mosquito than jeans. Another trick is to not wear perfume or after shave lotion or, for that matter, to shampoo your hair. No one knows why but certain scents also seem to be alluring to mosquitoes.

Why do mosquitoes bite?

Actually, not all mosquitoes bite. Males don't suck blood (they feed on plant juices), but most females must drink blood to get the protein they need to make eggs. One meal from you could make 50 to 100 eggs. A mosquito has a sharp "beak" that pierces a victim's skin. Once the skin is broken, the mosquito spits some saliva into the wound to prevent her victim's blood from clotting normally. This makes it easy for the mosquito to suck up blood without getting it stuck in her needlelike beak.

Do insects bleed?

Insects have blood, as you know if you've ever accidentally squished one between your fingers, so they do "bleed." But an insect's blood isn't as essential to it as our blood is to us. We human beings use our blood to carry nutrients through our bodies. An insect only uses its blood as padding between its internal organs (the heart, crop, stomach, etc.) and its skeleton, which is on the outside of its body. Because an insect's blood doesn't transfer nutrients to its organs it can't bleed to death the same way we can.

Is it true that a porcupine can shoot its quills?

An adult porcupine has about 30,000 light, hollow quills, which grow all over its body except on its face, legs, belly and the underside of its tail. On the quills' shafts are tiny barbs that stick into things, making them difficult to pull out. While a porcupine does not shoot its quills, it does use them as a weapon. When a porcupine is mad or frightened, it turns its back on its enemy, makes its quills stand on end and shakes its tail. Often the attacker will be hit by the tail and some quills will stick in its body.

A porcupine's quills are not poisonous, but they may slowly work their way through the attacker's body, possibly causing infection. The porcupine, meanwhile, ambles on its way, growing new quills to replace the old.

Is it true that you get warts if you touch a toad?

You won't get warts if you touch a toad. Warts on human skin aren't caused by touching something; instead, they are caused by a virus that you catch. Although a toad's skin might look warty – and although its bumps are actually called "warts" – touching a toad won't make your skin look that way.

Nevertheless, toads do not make great playmates. For protection, they ooze out a poisonous liquid from two glands behind their eyes. If you get any of this on your hands and then touch your eyes or mouth, you'll feel a burning sensation. Needless to say, this is effective protection for toads. While a predator may eat one toad, the sensation is so awful it will probably never eat another!

Is a ladybug good luck? If so, why does the poem say it should fly away home?

Ladybugs are considered to be good luck by farmers because they eat pests such as plant lice (aphids), mealybugs and other insects that destroy farmers' plants and crops.

The chant about ladybugs came from Germany, where, after a farmer harvested a field of hops, it was customary to burn the vines to destroy pests and prepare the field for the next planting. Since baby ladybugs are wingless and therefore unable to fly, the farmers hoped the adults would whisk them away somehow to safety.

Is it true that ostriches hide their heads in the sand?

When a male ostrich sits on its nest, it sometimes lays its head flat on the sand, and since its head and long neck are sand colored, they almost disappear from sight. What's left sticking up – the ostrich's lovely feathery behind – looks so much like a bush that even the smartest predator is fooled.

Is it true that you can hear the sea in a seashell?

When you put a seashell up to your ear, you can hear a muffled roar that sounds just like the sea. If you cup your hand around your ear, you'll hear almost the same sound. The shape of the shell, or your cupped hand, traps the sound waves in the air and causes them to break up. What sounds like the rhythm of the sea pounding on the shore is really just a jumble of sounds getting smashed up. The best-shaped shell for special sound effects is the conch.

Is it true that a camel stores water in its hump?

Years ago people believed that because the camel could survive for days in the desert without drinking, its hump must contain water. We now know that this isn't so. The camel's hump contains fat – it's an energy storage tank for use when food is scarce.

Why is some hair straight while other hair is curly?

The curliness or straightness of your hair depends on its sensitivity to the effects of humidity and heat. If you cut a straight hair in half crosswise and look at it under a microscope, you'll see that it is perfectly circular, while a curly hair is oval. On humid days some hair changes shape slightly, which is why you might be one of those people whose hair is curly during the humid days of summer but straight during the winter.

Why are some people left-handed and others right-handed?

Different areas of your brain control different parts of your body. The right side of your brain controls the left side of your body and the left side controls the right. Since there's a limited amount of space in your brain and many actions, such as writing, require only one hand, your brain gears up one way or the other.

More people's brains tell them to be right-handed, but either is quite normal. How is it decided whether you'll be left- or right-handed? Here are two of many ideas: Some scientists believe this is something you inherit from a parent or grandparent; others believe that newborn children can use either hand just as well and it's chance that causes them to start using one or the other.

How does an inoculation keep you from getting measles?

When a doctor gives you a shot for measles, he or she is actually giving you a very mild infection of the measles. Usually this infection is so weak you don't even notice it, but your body does. It immediately begins to manufacture disease-fighters called antibodies. Once in your body, these antidisease antibodies stay there ready to fight off a real attack of measles if it ever comes along.

Why do feet smell?

The skin on your feet, like the rest of your skin, is covered with tiny sweat glands that are there to help you keep cool. These sweat glands ooze a liquid that is mostly water, but also contains some salt and a chemical called urea. It's the urea that causes the sweat to smell. Your feet don't sweat any more than your hands or armpits do, but because feet are usually wrapped up in socks and shoes most of the time, the sweat has nowhere to escape. It just collects all day, and when you take your shoes off – whew! P.S.: If you don't wash your feet often, bacteria start to grow on them and make them twice as whiffy.

Why does the sound of fingernails scratching on a blackboard bother us?

No one knows for sure why most of us find this screech so unpleasant, but here's one theory. The sound produced by scratching fingernails on a blackboard is very high pitched – high enough to make some people's ears hurt. And because it sounds like a shriek, our brains might unconsciously think it's also a threatening sound. The combination of pain and what we think is a danger signal is enough to make us jump when fingernails and blackboard connect.

How do you feel things?

All along the surface of your skin are tiny nerve ends. When your skin touches something gently, some of the nerve ends react, allowing you to determine the shape and texture of the object you've touched. Other nerve ends are pain receptors that, when injured or touched by something hot or cold, send messages about these things to your brain. Different areas of your body have different numbers of nerves, and because of this, your brain can be fooled.

For example, try this trick on a friend: press the ends of two pencils fairly close together on your friend's back. See if your friend can guess how many pencils you used. The answer will probably be one.

Why? Because the nerves that sense touch on your back are few and far apart, they can't send precise messages to your brain. See what happens when you try the trick on the pad of a friend's thumb. Was he or she fooled?

How much blood do we have in our body? If we give blood away, how do we get it back?

If you were to step on the scales, then drain off all the water in your body, you'd be taking away 70 percent of your weight. Of that 70 percent only 15 percent is actually blood. Put another way, a 68 kg/150 pound man has 5½ *l*/186 ounces of blood in his body. So 450 cc/15.2 ounces (which is all we donate at a time) is really very little in terms of the body's entire blood content.

Your body is like a factory that is always running smoothly. When it realizes that there's a sudden shortage of blood, this "factory" speeds up the work process because to get blood "back," your body has to make it. Your blood is made up of a straw-colored liquid called plasma, red cells, white cells and platelets. Once you've given blood, fluids already in your body and those you drink after donating quickly help to form new plasma. To replace red and white cells, many different areas of the body go on overtime. Red cells are primarily replaced by bone marrow; white cells are replaced from many sources, including the lymph glands, as well as bone marrow; and the liver manufactures the proteins, albumins and globulins we need. The entire refuelling job from the loss of 450 cc/15.2 ounces of blood takes about two weeks.

Why are all babies born with blue eyes?

All babies – even animal babies – are born with pale, colorless eyes, but their irises look blue because of the way the light reflects off them. Eye colors, like the colors in your paintbox, are made by a substance called "pigment." Babies begin to produce pigment when they're born, but it takes a few days or weeks before there's enough to make a definite color show up in the eyes.

Where does the water go when the tide goes out?

Did you guess that it rushes over to the far shore? Well, it doesn't. It rises up into an enormous bulge that is spread out over such a wide area you wouldn't be able to see it even if you were sitting in a satellite directly over the ocean. If you sat beside a pail of water at the beach you wouldn't be able to see the water bulge up in the pail, either, because that area is too small. Scientists, however, have been able to prove that the water bulges by using satellites equipped with remote sensing devices. These devices that measure the distance between the water and the satellite detect even the slightest height variation in the water below.

Why does this bulge happen? The answer has to do with the moon. The moon's gravity, acting like a powerful magnet, pulls the water on the side of the earth that's closest to the moon into a bulge. And because the earth turns in a complete circle during every 24-hour period, this water bulge moves across the earth's surface. When the bulge meets land, it makes a high tide; when it's far away from land, it causes a low tide.

Amazing though it seems, when it's high tide on one side of the earth it's also high tide on the other side of the earth. How? It sounds unbelievable, but while the moon is busy pulling water toward it on one side of the earth, it's also pulling the earth away from the water—on the opposite side.

How can you tell how far away a thunderstorm is?

To find out how far away a thunderstorm is, count the number of seconds between the lightning flash and the sound of thunder and divide by three. This will tell you approximately how many kilometers away the lightning struck. (If it's miles you're more comfortable with, divide by five.) If the flash and the thunder happen together, you won't need any math to tell you that the storm is directly overhead. Your ears will be ringing from the tremendous crack.

68

What are lightning and thunder?

When you see a flash of lightning dart across the sky, what you're seeing is an electrical discharge that happens between two charge centers, one positive and the other negative. These two centers can be two clouds, or a cloud and the ground, or even just one cloud if all the positive particles are in one area of that cloud and all the negative ones are in another area of the same cloud.

When lightning bolts flash through the air they heat up the area they pass through. Thunder is the sound wave produced by the rapid expansion of air that's been suddenly heated up by the lightning bolt.

If clouds are filled with water, how can they float?

Clouds are made up of tiny water droplets so small that they can only be seen with a microscope. These minidrops don't weigh much, so they—and therefore a cloud of them—can be kept aloft by warm air rising from the earth. But when many of these droplets cling together, forming a large drop of water, they're too heavy to stay up. When that happens, it's time to get out your umbrella.

Where does dew come from?

You can make your own dew just by taking a cold pitcher of water out of the refrigerator on a hot day. Tiny beads of water, like the beads you see on grass on summer mornings, form on the outside of the pitcher. When warm, moist air touches the cold pitcher—or the cold grass—the air cools down too. Cool air can't hold as much moisture as warm air, so some of the water drops out onto the cold surface.

What are UFOs?

A UFO (unidentified flying object) is anything in the sky that's unexplained and behaves in a way that seems unusual. Many things average people see in the sky are unexplained and, therefore, are called UFOs. However, to an astronomer or a meteorologist, these same things might have a logical explanation. They might be airplanes, or research balloons reflecting sunlight, or the planet Venus, whose light can be distorted by heat waves in the atmosphere.

Some scientists think that all UFO sightings (it's estimated that there are at least 100 reported world-wide every day) can be explained in such simple terms. Others think they cannot and insist that there are many reports that remain unexplained even after investigation by experts. One of their possible explanations for UFOs is that they are flying saucers; another is that they are some kind of weather or atmospheric event, such as ball lightning, which appears as if from nowhere and then disappears. Yet another idea is that UFOs exist only in the mind of the person seeing them. Think about that!

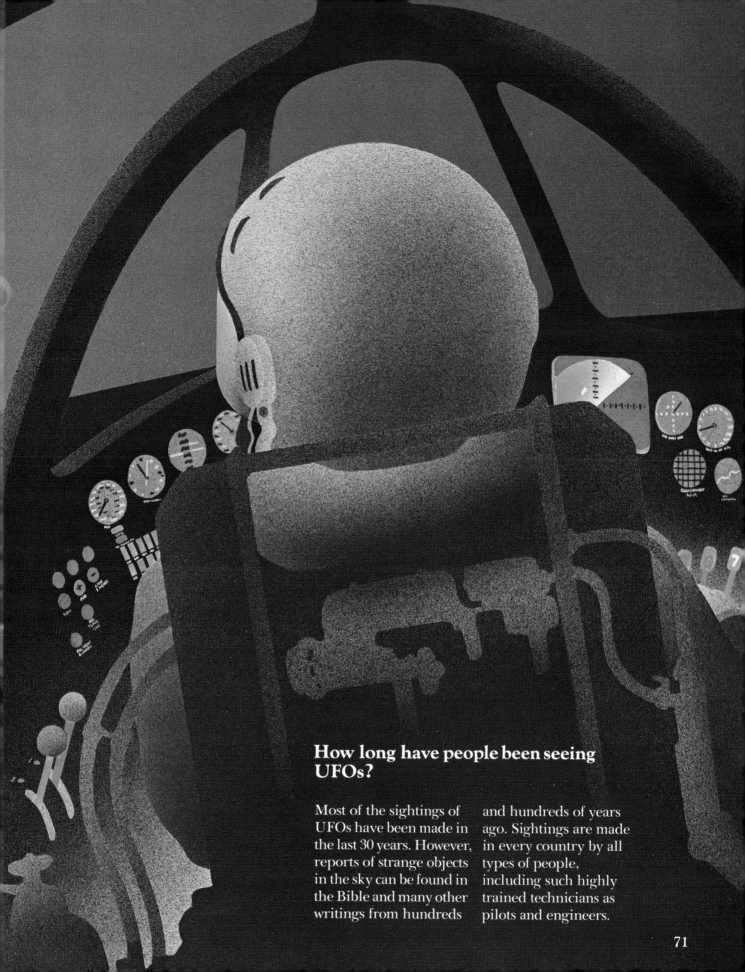

How long have people been seeing UFOs?

Most of the sightings of UFOs have been made in the last 30 years. However, reports of strange objects in the sky can be found in the Bible and many other writings from hundreds and hundreds of years ago. Sightings are made in every country by all types of people, including such highly trained technicians as pilots and engineers.

What are planets?

By definition, a planet is any large body in our solar system that orbits around the sun. The Earth is a planet, and there are eight others. In order, they are Mercury, Venus, Earth, Mars, Jupiter, Saturn, Uranus, Neptune and Pluto. The orbits are rather like rings around a bull's eye, with the bull's eye being the sun. Mercury orbits closest to the sun, Pluto the farthest away (although sometimes it gets inside Neptune's orbit). Jupiter is the largest planet, 12 times the diameter of the Earth.

Pluto is the smallest— smaller than Earth's moon.

It is possible that beyond Pluto, but still in our solar system, there is a planet bigger than the Earth, or that other stars like the sun could have planets, but we haven't discovered them because they are so far away.

Why is Venus called our twin planet?

Venus is a dead planet of scorched brown rock. Above the Venusian ground swirls a soupy, orange smog topped by poisonous clouds of sulfuric acid that are swept around the planet nonstop by strong winds. It might seem hard to understand why people call this our twin planet.

Venus was named our twin partly because it's the same size as Earth and is our next-door neighbor in the solar system. But recently scientists have begun to wonder if Venus was once much more like Earth than it is today— complete with rivers, streams and maybe even vegetation.

Venus is closer to the sun than Earth is. Some new theories suggest that this closeness to the sun caused Venus to heat up billions of years ago. The oceans evaporated there boosting the carbon dioxide in the Venusian atmosphere. This increased carbon dioxide made the atmosphere thicker so that it trapped even more heat. Once this happened, the planet became so hot that all possibility of life died. But before all scientists can accept this theory about our now-unalike twin, much more must be known.

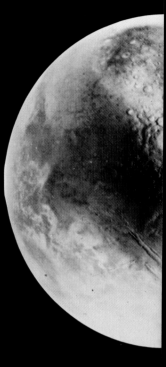

If you visited a planet with several moons, could you see them all in the sky at the same time?

The planets Mars, Jupiter, Saturn, Uranus and Neptune all have more than one moon, although some of them are very small. If you were to travel to Jupiter you'd find it an exciting place to look for moons. Four of Jupiter's moons would look somewhat the same as our one moon and there would be times when all four could be seen at once, each in a different phase. But the best place of all for moon-watching would be Saturn. If you looked into the sky from Saturn on a clear night, you might see at least five of Saturn's seven moons.

How can the moon shine when it's dark?

The moon shines all the time, even during the day, but you can see it better at night just as a lamp seems brighter at night than at noon. Why does the moon shine nonstop like this? It's like a gigantic mirror in the sky, reflecting the sun's light back to earth.

Why does the moon look larger when it's close to the horizon?

Before thinking about that, look at this drawing and decide which toy soldier looks the largest. Most people would say the one on the right. Because other things in the picture make that soldier look farther away, your brain thinks he's taller than the others. But measure the soldiers and you'll find they're exactly the same size. You were fooled.

When you can see the moon at the same time as other things – such as buildings, mountains, trees and so on – it looks larger for the same reason. But if you hold up your little finger at arm's

What is the moon made of?

When the astronauts traveled to the moon, they gathered rocks and dirt from the surface and brought the samples back to earth in special boxes. Scientists who have studied this material say that the moon is made mostly of material similar to basalt, the most common type of rock we have on earth. But the basalt on the moon has been mostly smashed into gravellike rubble by meteorites crashing into the moon for millions of years.

Why do stars fall?

If you watch carefully on a dark night when there are lots of stars in the sky, every once in a while you may see what looks like a star falling quickly. Then it disappears. Although some people call this phenomenon a falling star or a shooting star, it isn't a star at all. What "fell" was a peanut-sized meteor – a bit of rubble sailing around in outer space. Meteors, which are out there by the trillion, travel 100 times faster than a jet aircraft. If they happen to come close to the earth, they rub against atoms in our atmosphere, which causes so much heat that the meteors usually burn up before they hit the ground.

Why do people float in outer space?

If you have ever bounced on a trampoline, or felt a sinking feeling in your stomach when flying in an airplane during turbulence, you have some idea of what it feels like to be floating in outer space. At the highest point of your bounce, you get a strange feeling of weightlessness, as if you are floating.

Rocketships that carry astronauts into space work like a trampoline. They are powerful enough to keep you traveling at a speed that escapes the force of the earth's gravity. Thus the astronauts, and everything else not anchored down in the ship, "floats" around. How fast a spaceship must be going for its astronauts to escape from the earth's gravity and feel weightless is determined by how far out the craft is in space – and thus how far it is from the effect of the earth's pull. If you take off from other planets or the moon, which also have gravity that pulls things toward them, your spaceship has to go fast enough to counteract their gravitational pull also.

There is a mid-point between the earth and the moon where neither's gravity affects the spaceship, so even if the craft were stopped, the astronauts would still feel weightless. It's only when the rocket's engines are fired that the astronauts are pushed back against their chairs, just as you are when your plane takes off.

If there's no air in space, what is there?

Higher than about 32 km/20 miles above the ground, there's hardly any air, and far out in space there isn't any at all. That's why it's called space – it's almost completely empty. Special instruments on spacecraft have found a few specks of dust, as well as some atoms thrown off the sun by solar flares and some fast-moving particles called cosmic rays. But there are so few of these that you wouldn't notice them if you were right out there in space with them. In fact, all you would see is blackness – and thousands of stars.

INDEX

PHOTO and ILLUSTRATION CREDITS

pp. 4-5 Stouffer Enterprises/Animals Animals (cedar waxwings);
6-9 Olena Kassian;
10-11 Kim LaFavre, Olena Kassian;
12-13 Olena Kassian, Elaine Macpherson, Anker Odum;
14-15 Michael C.T. Smith/ Photo Researchers, Inc. (emperor penguin);
16-17 Stouffer Enterprises/ Animals Animals (cedar waxwings), Townsend P. Dickinson/Photo Researchers, Inc. (arctic tern), Ted Levin/Animals Animals (Atlantic puffin);
18-19 Patti Murray/Animals Animals (anhinga), Fred Unverhau/Animals Animals (screech owl);
20-21 Lynda Cooper;
22-23 Tony Thomas;
24-25 Lynda Cooper;
26-27 S.C. Bisserot/Bruce Coleman Inc.;
28-29 M.P.L. Fogden/Bruce Coleman Inc.;
30-33 Tina Holdcroft;
34-35 Tony Thomas;
36-37 Hans Reinhard/Bruce Coleman Inc.;
38-41 Olena Kassian;
42-43 Wolfgang Bayer/Bruce Coleman Inc. (background diver), William H. Amos/ Bruce Coleman Inc. (jelly-fish), Harry Hartman/ Bruce Coleman Inc. (shells), Jane Burton/Bruce Coleman Inc. (female seahorse), Ron and Valerie Taylor/Bruce Coleman Inc. (oyster), Tom McHugh/Photo Researchers, Inc. (electric eel), Kjell B. Sandved/Bruce Coleman Inc. (starfish).
44-45 Olena Kassian;
46-47 Tina Holdcroft;
48-49 Fred Bruemmer (walrus), Tom McHugh/ Photo Researchers, Inc. (stingray), Lynn M. Stone/ Animals Animals (domestic hog), Ted Walker/Animals Animals (whale spouting), Olena Kassian (camel), Michael and Barbara Reed/ Animals Animals (Pekinese), Peter Swan (caribou);
50-51 Lynda Cooper;
52-53 Elaine Macpherson, Lynda Cooper, Mary Carrick, Olena Kassian;
54-57 Tina Holdcroft;
58-61 Julian Mulock;
62-63 Dwight Kuhn;
64-67 Tina Holdcroft;
68-69 John Foster;
70-71 Clive Dobson/Fifty Fingers Inc.;
72-73 NASA;
74-75 Arthur Holbrook/ Miller Services Limited.
Front Cover: Nigel Dickson

CONSULTANTS

J.F. Alex, *Department of Environmental Biology, University of Guelph;*

Roy Anderson, *Department of Zoology, University of Guelph;*

Allan Baker, *Curator, Department of Ornithology, Royal Ontario Museum;*

Ian Barker, *Department of Pathology, Ontario Veterinary College, University of Guelph;*

Peter Beamish, *Ceta-Research;*

Ron Brooks, *Department of Zoology, University of Guelph;*

John Burton, *Department of Animal and Poultry Science, University of Guelph;*

Centre for UFO Studies, *Evanston, Illinois;*

Jim Dick, *Department of Ornithology, Royal Ontario Museum;*

Terry Dickinson, *Astronomy Specialist;*

James Eckenwalder, *Department of Botany, University of Toronto;*

John Grayson, *Department of Physiology, Faculty of Medicine, University of Toronto;*

Peter Hallett, *Department of Physiology, Faculty of Medicine, University of Toronto;*

R. Herst, *Red Cross Blood Transfusion Clinic;*

Herzberg Institute of Astrophysics, *Ottawa, Ontario;*

Bruce Hunter, *Department of Clinical Studies, University of Guelph;*

Ross James, *Department of Ornithology, Royal Ontario Museum;*

Finn Larsen, *Vancouver Public Aquarium;*

Ross MacCulloch, *Department of Ichthyology and Herpetology, Royal Ontario Museum;*

Brian Marshall, *Department of Entomology, Royal Ontario Museum;*

Susan McIver, *Department of Zoology, University of Toronto;*

Angus McKinnon, *Department of Clinical Studies, University of Guelph;*

D.H. Osmond, *Department of Physiology, Faculty of Medicine, University of Toronto;*

John Parker, *Toronto General Hospital;*

Arlene Reiss, *Department of Vertebrate Palaeontology, Royal Ontario Museum;*

Robert Schemenauer, *Environment Canada;*

Morris Smith, *Department of Environmental Biology, University of Guelph;*

Victor Springer, *Smithsonian Institute;*

Ian Stirling, *Canadian Wildlife Service;*

R.W. Stonehouse, *the cat doctor;*

Thomas Swatland, *Department of Animal and Poultry Science, University of Guelph;*

Michael Thompson, *Department of Chemistry, University of Toronto;*

Elizabeth Wilson, *Department of Clinical Studies, University of Guelph;*

Patrick Woo, *Department of Zoology, University of Guelph.*